Philosop...
the essential study g...

Philosophy: The Essential Study Guide is a compact and straight-forward handbook to the skills needed to study philosophy, aimed at anyone coming to the subject for the first time or just looking to improve their performance. Nigel Warburton, bestselling author of *Philosophy: The Basics*, clarifies what is expected of students and offers strategies and guidance to help them make effective use of their study time and improve their marks.

Readers who put his principles into practice will improve their ability to:

- **read** philosophy – both skimming and in-depth analysis of historical and contemporary work, understanding the examples and terminology used
- **listen** to philosophy – formal lectures and informal classroom teaching, preparation, picking up on arguments used, note taking
- **discuss** philosophy – arguing and exploring, asking questions, communicating in concise and understandable ways
- **write** philosophy – planning and researching essays and other written tasks, thinking up original examples, avoiding plagiarism

Written in Nigel Warburton's customary student-friendly style and filled with sound advice and top tips, *Philosophy: The Essential Study Guide* is an indispensable guide for all students of the subject.

Nigel Warburton is the author of *Philosophy:The Basics* (4th edition), *Philosophy: The Classics* (2nd edition), *Thinking from A to Z* (2nd edition) and *The Art Question*, and editor of *Philosophy: Basic Readings* (2nd edition), all published by Routledge.

NIGEL WARBURTON

Philosophy: the essential study guide

Routledge
Taylor & Francis Group

LONDON AND NEW YORK

First published 2004
by Routledge
11 New Fetter Lane, London EC4P 4EE

Simultaneously published in the USA and Canada
by Routledge
29 West 35th Street, New York, NY 10001

Routledge is an imprint of the Taylor & Francis Group

© 2004 Nigel Warburton

Typeset in Rotis by Keystroke, Jacaranda Lodge, Wolverhampton
Printed and bound in Great Britain by MPG Books Ltd, Bodmin

British Library Cataloguing in Publication Data
A catalogue record for this book is available from the British Library

Library of Congress Cataloging in Publication Data
Warburton, Nigel, 1962–
    Philosophy : the essential study guide / Nigel Warburton
        p. cm.
    Includes bibliographical references (p.   ).
    1. Philosophy–Study and teaching.   I. Title.
B52.W375 2004
107'.1–dc22   2003027982

ISBN 0–415–34179–5 (hbk)
ISBN 0–415–34180–9 (pbk)

Contents

Contents

Introduction

Students beginning a course in philosophy are often confused about what is expected of them. This short book should clarify this. If you put its principles into practice you will make more effective use of your study time, and in the process become a better thinker.

I am very grateful for comments from Tony Bruce, Michael Clark, Stephen Law, Anna Motz, my copy-editor Christine Firth and several anonymous publisher's readers on an earlier draft of this book. I am also very grateful to all the students who, without realising it, helped me write this.

'Some people would sooner die than think. In fact they do.'

Bertrand Russell

Philosophy isn't a spectator sport

The main thing to remember when you are studying philosophy is that it is not a spectator sport. You have to engage with philosophical ideas as a philosopher and not simply as a reporter writing up the issues at a distance. Studying philosophy involves learning to philosophise. That is an essential part of the process. In this way it differs from, for example, the study of poetry. Usually when you study poetry you are not required or expected to write as a poet. You learn how to be a good critic of poetry. But you do not write your criticism *as* poetry. You can study the sonnet without actually writing one. Similarly when you study art history you don't usually do this by putting paint onto canvas. You learn to look at paintings (and sculpture and buildings) and to understand these in their historical context. With philosophy, every philosophy essay is itself a piece of philosophy. You are expected to argue for your conclusion. You needn't produce something startlingly original. But it must be well argued. You are making a case for your position, just as the great philosophers of the past have made cases for their positions. You are engaged in the same sort of activity as them – explaining, interpreting, criticising, putting forward ideas. In this respect philosophy is like the practical aspects of the sciences: someone doing an experiment in physics, for example, is engaged in the same sort of activity as the great physicists of the past have been. Similarly, when studying history, you may do your own piece of historical research. In philosophy you can't avoid philosophising.

The same is true when you are reading, listening to or discussing philosophy. You will be reading *as* a philosopher (i.e. in a critically engaged mode) and listening *as* a philosopher (thinking through the implications and possible responses to what is being said). When discussing philosophy you will be engaged in philosophical debate, not simply in debates *about* philosophy. This is part of what makes philosophy such an exciting and challenging subject to study. It's not a matter of just learning what other people have thought, so much as learning to think as a philosopher yourself. In a real sense studying philosophy is a process of *becoming* a philosopher. Any serious study of philosophy will involve learning what other philosophers have said, and something of the context in which they said it. But this is not usually an end in itself. When we study philosophy's past as philosophers we do not visit a museum of dry and dusty ideas. We study philosophy's past in order to contribute to present-day philosophy or at least to understand where the problems we study now originate.

If, within a philosophy department, you take a course on the seventeenth-century philosopher, René Descartes, for example, you will probably be expected to engage with his ideas about scepticism and what we can know for certain. You will probably also study his famous 'Cogito', the notion that having thoughts proves that you exist. You won't simply learn facts about his intellectual and historical context, or the main events of his life, just for the sake of it. The point of studying the historical and biographical background is that it will help you understand what Descartes was trying to communicate, the kinds of ideas he was reacting against, the dominant models available to him at the time, and so on. Nor will you focus exclusively on the literary merits of his writing. All these aspects of Descartes, his context and his writing style have their part to play in a serious philosophical study of Descartes. But the ultimate aim is to understand and engage with his arguments, arguments which provide a starting point for many present-day philosophical discussions and which certainly had an immense impact on his successors.

If you are taking a course in philosophy, then, you are in training to become a philosopher. The history of ideas is only likely to form a part of your studies. And it is not typically an end in itself. Philosophy is primarily an activity, not a body of knowledge: that is one reason why it is such a vibrant and exciting subject. Many of the skills you acquire and develop are transferable to other areas of philosophy and beyond. If you study philosophy it is likely to colour your thought for the rest of your life.

The thinker and the mere scholar

The truth that has been merely learnt sticks to us like an artificial limb, a false tooth, a nose of wax, or at best like a rhinoplastic nose formed from someone else's flesh. On the other hand, the truth acquired through our own thinking is like the natural limb; it alone really belongs to us. On this rests the distinction between the thinker and the mere scholar. The intellectual gain of the man who thinks for himself is, therefore, like a beautiful painting that vividly stands out with correct light and shade, sustained tone, and perfect harmony of colours. The intellectual acquisition of the mere scholar, on the other hand, is like a large palette full of bright

5

colours, systematically arranged perhaps, but without harmony,
sequence, and significance.

Arthur Schopenhauer, 'On Thinking for Oneself'

There are four principal ways in which we learn to philosophise. If you want to succeed at philosophy, which ultimately means if you want to become a good philosopher, then you will need to develop these four habits. They are habits which will help you whatever subject you study:

- Active reading
- Active listening
- Active discussion
- Active writing

It is through the combination of these four habits that most philosophers have developed their philosophical skills. There are notable exceptions, such as Socrates who, as far as we can tell, never wrote any philosophy, but achieved his status as a great philosopher through the power of his intellect in discussion. And someone who is profoundly deaf can still become a great philosopher, despite not being able to engage in active listening except through lip-reading or simultaneous signing or subtitles. Typically, however, philosophy students master their subject through the combination of these four activities.

Notice the stress on *active* rather than *passive* reading, listening, discussion and writing. As I have already emphasised, philosophy should not be thought of as a spectator sport, but rather as a demanding, and sometimes exhilarating, *practice*. Your aim should be to think more clearly, and to learn from the highest achievements of those who have already thought philosophically about the topics you examine.

As with most activities, philosophy becomes easier to do when you have learnt the basic manoeuvres, and practised them. It is very easy to become stale as a thinker; one of the surest ways of doing this is to relax into a passive mode, simply memorising and regurgitating what others have said to you, speaking and writing without really thinking. Some people never rise above this state. Once you have learnt to be active and engaged in your thought and writing, though, you should be able to apply this to many aspects of your life. People who have studied philosophy often describe it as the subject above all others which has given them the strength to think things through critically for themselves. They no longer accept others' opinions unquestioningly. They want to elicit, investigate and perhaps challenge reasons given in support of those opinions. They are alive to ideas. They write with real force because they have learnt to marshall arguments in support of a conclusion, even when dealing with highly abstract and difficult subject matter. In this way, the active study of philosophy can be a rewarding and empowering experience.

> Education can be unimaginative. It can be a straightjacket, making you efficient in the three Rs [i.e. Reading, wRiting and aRithmetic], but the tools are lacking to make thinking and analysis more important. You don't learn to be critical. If I have made anything of my life, it has been because philosophy has enabled me to do so.
>
> Michael Mansfield QC, top barrister

Habit 1: Active reading

> To read good books is like holding a conversation with the most eminent minds of past centuries, and moreover, a studied conversation in which these authors reveal to us only the best of their thoughts.
>
> René Descartes, *Discourse on Method*

Although it is exciting and inspiring to engage with the ideas of some of the greatest thinkers known to humanity, and to read about some of life's most profound questions, it can also be daunting. At some point in your studies you will be assigned to read articles or books which at first glance (and often at second, third, fourth and fifth glance too, if you have the energy to keep going back to them) make no sense whatsoever. Don't be put off by this. What you may not realise is that we all find some philosophical writing difficult to follow, even those of us who have been studying the subject for twenty years or more. If anyone tells you they have never had any difficulty in following the thread of a philosophical article or book, then they are certainly either lying or deceiving themselves. Philosophy can be a challenging subject to study. It is for the most part an abstract subject. This can make it extremely difficult to keep track of chains of argument. Reading philosophy is not a matter of grazing on facts, but rather of grappling with what may seem quite obscure ideas. If the work you are reading was written some time ago, these ideas may be expressed in archaic language. It is likely to include technical terms, or familiar words used in unfamiliar ways. And, it has to be admitted, not all philosophers worth studying write clearly. Some even seem to delight in the obscurity of their writing.

There are, however, several strategies that can give you a better chance of understanding the texts you need to read.

Don't be passive

Reading is sometimes an ingenious device for avoiding thought.
Sir Arthur Helps, *Friends in Council*

It is a mistake to think of reading as passive. It is an activity. You need to think about and question what you are reading, not just absorb someone else's ideas. If you engage critically with whatever you read, you will understand it more thoroughly and remember it better. It will be alive for you, and have some meaning. You won't think of it as something you have to learn by heart to pass an examination, but rather as a stimulus to your own thought about issues that matter to you. If you just let your eyes run over the words, without really interacting with what you read, then what you are reading will probably remain dead for you. It will seem dry and obscure and it will probably eventually send you to sleep.

Reading is to the mind what exercise is to the body.
Richard Steele

To be an effective student you will need to retain some of the ideas you read: memory does have a part to play in the study of philosophy. But unless you understand and are engaged by the issues, you are unlikely to remember very much. And even if you manage to parrot ideas, that won't get you very far in this subject. Once you get into the habit of active reading, however, you will start to understand philosophy in the spirit in which it was written.

I should not like my writing to spare other people the trouble of thinking. But, if possible to stimulate someone to thoughts of his own.
Ludwig Wittgenstein, foreword *to Philosophical Investigations*

How can you go about reading actively? One way is to take notes as you read. You needn't think of these as something that you will archive for later consultation. You can take notes to help you keep track of key points. You can pick out passages that you find particularly interesting, inspiring or important. You can jot down your own doubts and objections to what you read, perhaps, if you own the book or article, in the margins of the text you are reading. You can also discuss your reading later with other students. Leave yourself time to stop and think through what you have just read. Reading philosophy in this active way is a much slower process than reading a novel or a newspaper. You need to develop good habits in this respect. If you treat philosophical writing as just something to skim and get the gist of without going any deeper, you will never make much progress in the subject.

Another way of avoiding passivity as you read is to ask yourself not just 'What does the author mean?' but 'Is the author right?' This can be a difficult question to answer. However, as a philosopher it is the basic question you should ask. Ultimately the point of reading other philosophers is to find out whether or not they were right. We also want to know if they were right for the right reasons; and if they were wrong, *why* they were wrong? We are interested in getting as close as we can to the truth on any issue. Our best hope for truth is a well-argued and well-supported case for a conclusion. In some cases we discover that we have been asking the wrong sort of question. Our best hope for progress in philosophy, however, is always through reasoning. We look at arguments, counterarguments, seek alternative explanations, or more streamlined theories. It is not enough that we might agree with a thinker's conclusion. We want to know if that thinker arrived at that conclusion by a reliable form of reasoning. For a philosopher, then, it should always matter whether or not an author is right about an issue and whether his or her conclusion is well supported by the arguments and evidence given.

There are several aspects to consider here. First, are the author's fundamental assumptions true? If someone argues logically from the assumption that everything written in *Genesis* is true, they may argue impeccably from a logical angle. But if the basic premise that everything written in *Genesis* is true is, as I believe, false, if for example, the world was not created in six days, we cannot be sure that any of their conclusions are true (nor can we be sure that they are false on the basis of the argument alone). Work out what the author's fundamental assumptions are, and ask yourself whether these assumptions are true or not. Then, consider the author's reasoning. Do the author's conclusions really follow from the argument given? Are there, perhaps, counterarguments and counterexamples that the author should have considered? Is the author guilty of making sweeping generalisations, or, perhaps of arguing on the basis of a single case? This involves asking these sorts of questions as you read and re-read. Learning to read actively and critically is an important part of a philosophical education.

This doesn't mean, however, that you should simply dismiss articles and books that make false assumptions and use faulty reasoning. Learning about others' positions challenges complacency and dogmatism. It can also help you refine your thinking skills. It can stimulate you to think through the reasons for your beliefs and in some cases be the catalyst for a change in beliefs. Many great philosophers were inspired to think deeply about issues in reaction to other thinkers with whom they disagreed. Some of Aristotle's ideas, for instance, arose directly from his disagreements with Plato; some of Immanuel Kant's thoughts were triggered by his reading of David Hume's work; most of Ludwig Wittgenstein's thought was developed in reaction to what he believed to be a misleading account of the mind.

Until you have had your views opposed, you will very likely hold them as prejudices, which you have never thought to defend. Under critical attack, if you are prepared to think for yourself, you may find that you gain a greater understanding of what you actually believe. You may even modify your views.

John Stuart Mill on the value of having your ideas challenged

> Both teachers and learners go to sleep at their post as soon as there is no enemy in the field
>
> *On Liberty*

> ... even if the received opinion be not only true, but the whole truth; unless it is suffered to be, and actually is, vigorously and earnestly contested, it will, by most of those who receive it, be held in the manner of a prejudice, with little comprehension or feeling of its rational grounds. And not only this, but ... the meaning of the doctrine itself will be in danger of being lost or enfeebled, and deprived of its vital effect on the character and conduct: the dogma becoming a mere formal profession, inefficacious for good, but cumbering the ground and preventing the growth of any real and heartfelt conviction from reason or personal experience.
>
> *On Liberty*

Get an overview

One way of finding your bearings when beginning to read a book, a chapter or an article is to get a sketchy overview of the whole piece. If you are reading a book, the title is the most obvious place to start: it should tell you something about the book's central theme. If you are reading a chapter or an article, its title, if it is well chosen, should give you an idea of the central topic and possibly the angle taken towards it. If you are assigned to read Willard Quine's 'Two Dogmas of Empiricism' for instance, the title should alert you to the fact that he is attacking two things; that these have been held up until then in a dogmatic rather than questioning way;

and that these things are central to Empiricism. It is fairly obvious from this title, too, that, by labelling these beliefs 'dogmas', Quine is about to call them into question rather than simply identify them.

Some titles are deliberately enigmatic. Compare two titles of articles by Thomas Nagel, 'Sexual Perversion' and 'What is it Like to be a Bat?', both reprinted in his *Mortal Questions*. The first title is directly informative: the subject of the paper is sexual perversion (though you may be surprised to learn that for Nagel the word 'perversion' does not imply any moral criticism). The second title is intriguing. It leaves the reader to do the work to find out why as a philosopher (rather than, say, as a zoologist) Nagel might want to investigate such a question. Even though it is an enigmatic title, it still gives the reader a clue as to the central theme of the article expressed through its main example (as will become clear if you read the article).

The back cover of a book may well give you a very brief indication of the key topics in the book and the angle taken by its author. Another good source of this information is the introduction: many authors use this to give you a map of the book as a whole, drawing attention to the main thread of their argument. The contents page can also be extremely useful, particularly if the author has used explanatory chapter headings: at the very least it provides you with an indication of the structure of the book. Conclusions of chapters, articles and books often restate the author's main arguments and conclusions. Don't be afraid to read the punchline of a book or article before you have looked at the main body of the text. Reading philosophy is not like reading a crime thriller. Far from spoiling the reading for you, you should find that knowing where the writer is heading helps you understand the structure of the argument.

If you know of any reviews of the book, these can give you a critical overview. The journal *Philosophical Books* is devoted entirely to reviews of recent books, and may be a useful resource for you. A well-written review should identify what, if anything, is distinctive and important about the book and will draw your attention to key passages and themes within it. It may be worth looking at entries about the author in dictionaries or encyclopedias of philosophy. These usually summarise the key themes of a philosopher's most important writings. Whenever possible consult several reference works rather than just one. That will give you a better overview of a philosopher's work.

Don't get bogged down in details

When you turn to the text itself, don't worry if you don't understand everything you read first time around. You will need to re-read most philosophy several times if you want to understand it thoroughly. And even after that, some aspects of an article or book can remain elusive. For a first reading, go through to the end of a difficult piece, skimming over incomprehensible passages. Then go back and begin again. You will be surprised how quickly what seemed obscure can start to become clear. If you read slowly, trying to make sense of everything you read, you may well lose track of what the main point is. It is a much more economical use of your time to go for the sketchy overview first, then read through quickly, skimming where necessary. Pay particular attention to the first and last paragraphs: as already mentioned, these often contain succinct overviews of the structure of a piece, its main conclusion or its angle on a topic. Finally, return to the piece, reading more thoroughly. Don't be demoralised if you still can't understand everything there. It may be that you are tired or preoccupied and need a break.

The quality of your reading is far more important than the total number of hours of study you put in. This is obvious, but some students order their time according to a work ethic that suggests that all they have to do is put in the appropriate number of hours at a desk for their study to be effective. Of course, you do need to allocate yourself sufficient time to read, bearing in mind too that reading speeds for philosophy tend to be much slower than reading speeds for other subjects. But it is far better to take a twenty-minute break from your reading and then return refreshed, than to slog on, nodding over your books, and not taking anything in. Several major philosophers did much of their thinking while walking. Thomas Hobbes even designed a cane with a place to store writing materials so that he could record ideas while out walking. Going for a walk between reading sessions is an excellent way of refreshing yourself. You may want to go through the ideas you have just been reading about while walking. If you are athletic, running, swimming or going to the gym can serve the same purpose.

Look for signposts

Good writers provide signposts. These usually occur at the beginning of paragraphs. They typically indicate what that section of the piece of writing is about. For example, in the chapter of John Stuart Mill's *On Liberty* that argues against censoring thought and its expression, Mill gives four main arguments in defence of his conclusion. He begins a paragraph: 'First, the opinion which it is attempted to suppress by authority may possibly be true. Those who desire to suppress it, of course, deny its truth; but they are not infallible' (Mill, *On Liberty*, Penguin edn, p. 77). These two sentences summarise the main point that Mill goes on to explain, elaborate and defend in the next few pages of the chapter. Because he has provided us with this signpost which clearly indicates that the target of his attack is the implicit claim of infallibility made by those who censor others' expression, it is relatively easy to understand the discussion that follows. Without such a signpost some readers would get lost, and be unsure whether this was the point that was being made, or whether what followed was a continuation of an earlier point. Look out for this kind of signpost. You might want to underline such sentences, as they reveal the structure of an author's thought. Once you become aware of how useful such sentences are to the reader trying to make sense of what's going on, you will be more likely to use similar signposts in your own writing.

Study tip

Whenever you come across a piece of philosophical writing which is particularly clear and well expressed, take the time to analyse what makes it so successful. Then apply your insights to your own writing. You may even find it useful to copy out an exceptionally powerful passage.

Make sure you know the point of any example used

One entertaining aspect of philosophy is the range of examples that philosophers use to make their points. Some philosophers, such as Daniel Dennett, Thomas Nagel, Robert Nozick, John Searle and Bernard Williams, are highly imaginative in their use of examples. It is very easy on a first reading to be seduced by the startling or compelling examples and entirely miss the point of how they function in the argument or what they are supposed to demonstrate. For example, in Robert Nozick's book, *Anarchy, State and Utopia*, he uses the following example:

> Suppose there were an experience machine that would give you any experience you desired. Superduper neuro-psychologists could stimulate your brain so that you would think and feel you were writing a great novel, or making a friend, or reading an interesting book. All the time you would be floating in a tank, with electrodes attached to your brain. Should you plug into this machine for life, pre-programming your life's experiences?
>
> (Robert Nozick, *Anarchy, State and Utopia*, p. 42)

Once you have read this passage, and the discussion of it that follows in Nozick's book, it is very hard to forget. It invites an imaginative reverie on the part of the reader. You may find yourself sidetracked into thinking about what you would want for yourself if you could programme a machine to give you the illusion of any experience you desired. In the process you may lose sense of what the point of the example is. Indeed, in this case, many students who have read this can give only a very hazy account of what precise point Nozick is making here. (In fact, he is using the thought experiment to demonstrate that for most of us some things matter more to us than how life feels from the inside. We, for example, want to engage with reality and not an illusion of it.) Whenever you encounter an example, make sure you know exactly what the writer is trying to get across. Don't allow yourself to drift off into a stream of consciousness about something loosely related to the main topic. Keep focused.

Look up key words in a dictionary of philosophy

If there are key words which occur several times in a chapter or article, make sure you understand what they mean. You can't hope to understand an article about, say, physicalism if you have no idea what the word 'physicalism' means in a philosophical context (it is the theory that the mind is a physical rather than non-physical thing). So look up such key words in one or more philosophical dictionaries. You don't need to look up every word that you are unsure of: that could slow your reading down to a point at which it is counterproductive. But if the same word or phrase keeps appearing, take the time to check it.

Although an ordinary dictionary can be useful in understanding unusual vocabulary, it won't help you much when reading philosophy. Dictionaries of philosophy are far more useful, as are introductory books that give a general overview of a topic and its key terms. Philosophers often use familiar words in unfamiliar or narrower ways. An ordinary dictionary is unlikely to be helpful with these specialised uses of familiar words. Philosophers often use technical terms that have been coined for use specifically within a philosophical context: for instance, within the philosophy of mind, 'interactionism' labels the theory that mind and body interact. Dictionaries of philosophy will provide you with explanations of such terms; ordinary dictionaries are likely to be misleading.

Learning to philosophise involves learning to understand and employ the vocabulary of the subject effectively. Some students find reading philosophy difficult because they haven't yet learnt the language of the subject. It is important to do this as early on in your philosophical career as possible. Then you will be able to appreciate and engage with what you read and hear. Unless you have a firm grasp of the vocabulary of philosophy much of the subject will pass you by.

Some foreign words used in philosophy

One reason why philosophy can be difficult to read is that philosophers often use foreign words. Sometimes these are unnecessary and exclude some readers. When writing, always use any standard English equivalent to the foreign word or phrase if possible. Some foreign words, however, are used as technical terms in philosophy and save a great deal of explanation. I have listed some of the more commonly used foreign words and phrases with brief explanations below.

a posteriori: literally, what comes after. In contrast to *a priori* knowledge, *a posteriori* knowledge can only be acquired and confirmed empirically. 'King Harold died at the battle of Hastings' is known *a posteriori*.

a priori: literally, what comes before. *A priori* knowledge is knowledge that does not depend on the use of the five senses for its authority. The senses will characteristically be involved in our coming to learn an *a priori* truth, but the evidence of the senses does not confirm the truth of it. *A priori* knowledge is contrasted with what is known *a posteriori*. Truths of mathematics are usually considered typical examples of truths known *a priori*. We know that $2 + 3 = 5$ not because we have repeatedly added two things to three things and come up with five things, but independently of this sort of experience.

ab initio: from the beginning.

Some foreign words used in philosophy

ad hoc: an *ad hoc* decision is one made for a one-off particular purpose rather than on the basis of a general rule.

ad hominem: literally, to the person. An *ad hominem* move in argument involves directing criticism at the source of the argument, the person, rather than the argument itself. This is a fallacious form of argument: in almost every case, attacking the person leaves the argument intact. There is a second rarer sense of *ad hominem*. This is the move of turning your opponent's argument back on him or herself. This move is an entirely legitimate appeal to consistency.

ad infinitum: to infinity.

akrasia: weakness of will.

angst: dread or anguish. A sense of unease about your life.

ceteris paribus: other things being equal.

cogito: literally means 'I think'. Usually used as shorthand for 'cogito ergo sum', which means 'I think therefore I exist'. Descartes used this argument, though not in these words, in his *Meditations*.

de facto: something that exists in fact, even though it has not been established by a law or principle.

de jure (sometimes written as *de iure*): in contrast to something that is established *de facto*, something established *de jure* is established according to a law or principle.

elenchus: the sort of questioning that Socrates engaged in to demonstrate how little people generally understand.

eudaimonia: although often translated as 'happiness', a more accurate translation of this Greek word used by Aristotle is 'flourishing'. It describes an ongoing state rather than a transient emotion.

ex nihilo: out of nothing, as in 'God created the universe *ex nihilo*'.

ibid.: there, in that place. Used to avoid repeating detailed references in footnotes. So the first reference might read 'Descartes, *Meditations* (Penguin edn p. 45).' After that subsequent quotations from the same book may be given as '*ibid.*, p. 33' *ibid.*, p. 46. etc.

idem: the same.

inter alia: among others.

ipso facto: from that very fact.

modus ponens: Latin phrase used to label 'affirming the antecedent' which is a technical name for an argument of the form:

> if p then q
> p
> therefore q

modus tollens: Latin phrase used to label 'denying the consequent' which is a technical name for an argument of the form:

> if p then q
> not q
> therefore not p

mutatis mutandis: making appropriate changes.

nescio quid: literally 'I know not what'.

non sequitur: literally 'it does not follow'. Sometimes spelt 'nonsequitur' (i.e. as one word rather than two). A *non sequitur* is a conclusion which does not follow logically from what has gone before.

pace: literally 'be at peace'. A phrase used, as in '*pace* Warburton' when the author wants to indicate that he or she is saying something that they know someone else would disagree with.

passim: throughout.

per se: by herself, himself, itself or themselves, i.e. intrinsically.

post hoc ergo propter hoc: literally 'after this , therefore because of this'. This phrase describes the unreliable form of reasoning that assumes that whatever happens after a particular event must be a causal consequence of that.

prima facie: at first glance.

qua: as. So for example in his role *qua* father he acted one way, but in his role *qua* headmaster, another.

quod erat demonstrandum or *QED*: which was to be demonstrated.

reductio ad absurdum: literally 'reduction to absurdity'. A form of argument which assumes the truth of what is being discussed and shows that it would lead directly to a contradiction.

sic: thus. This word is usually used to indicate that there is no typographical error or confusion in a quotation, but that this is really how it is meant to be expressed.

summum bonum: the greatest good.

tabula rasa: literally a blank slate. John Locke used this term to describe the newborn's mind on which sensory experience writes.

tu quoque: literally 'you too'. A form of argument in which the author demonstrates that his or her critic is also guilty of the fault that is being attributed to the author.

verbatim: word for word. A *verbatim* transcription does not alter a single word.

vice versa: the other way around.

weltanschauung: world view.

zeitgeist: spirit of the age.

Habit 2: Active listening

The formal lecture

The purest form of listening that you are likely to encounter when studying the subject occurs in the traditional lecture. Obviously the success of lectures depends on how skilled the lecturer is. But it also depends on the listening skills of the audience. For many students beginning the subject, philosophy lectures are daunting and confusing. Most students feel their attention wandering, and by the time they refocus on the lecture they have lost the thread of argument. Others try in vain to write down everything that is said, but, if they ever re-read their notes, cannot make any sense of them whatsoever. Many are bewildered by philosophical terminology and emerge blinking from the lecture hall unable to explain in the simplest terms what it was all about. When they look back at their notes they are just a series of doodles with odd words heavily underlined. The significance of the underlined words may have completely evaporated and the whole experience of the lecture have felt like a strange dream.

There are several reasons why talk about philosophy can be difficult to follow. First, unlike with most science teaching, there are relatively few facts that have to be learned in philosophy, and those which you do need to learn are usually best communicated in books or articles. So it is quite unusual to need to copy down large amounts of factual information during philosophy lectures. Most philosophers are intent on helping you to achieve a better understanding of the topic they are addressing, and so spend a great deal of the time explaining and illustrating points. If they want to give you detailed factual information they may well do this by giving you a printed handout, or writing facts out on a board or overhead projector for you. For students whose background is in fact-heavy subjects, like history or biology, it can be difficult to adjust. For most philosophy professors, the main aims are to stimulate you to think during lectures, and to motivate you to go on thinking, reading and discussing outside the lecture theatre. Ideally you should emerge from the lecture theatre with a better understanding of the topic covered, and a strong motivation to find out more about it. A good lecture will also have given you solid advice about the best books and articles on the topic and some sense of the angle taken in them.

Listening tip

As with reading, make sure you identify the point of any examples used in a lecture.

Another feature of philosophy that can make it difficult to follow aurally is that it typically operates at an abstract level. A philosopher won't usually be so interested in addressing the question of whether it was morally wrong to censor a particular video, but rather in more general questions such as 'Is censorship always wrong?' or 'What are acceptable grounds for censorship?' Particular cases serve to illustrate more general points or provide counterexamples which undermine generalisations. It can be difficult at first to see the relationship between more abstract general points being made and the particular examples used to make them.

Listening tip

It is often useful to take notes simply to help you follow the argument in the lecture. You may even want to throw the notes away at the end of the lecture. Even if you do, they will still have served a useful purpose if they focused your attention on the key elements of the argument and reminded you what the point of a discussion was when your mind began to wander or your head began to nod.

Pay attention to arguments

A further feature of philosophy worth emphasising is that it relies on argument. Not argument in the sense of dispute, but rather in the sense of making a case by giving reasons and evidence which lead to a conclusion. To follow an argument through to its conclusion you need to follow each step. If your attention drifts and you miss a step, it may be very difficult to see how the conclusion is supposed to follow from the premises. When philosophy lecturers are setting out arguments it is, then, particularly important that students follow each step of the reasoning process. Again, jotting down notes to help you follow what is going on may be useful.

Philosophy lectures may also, of course, be hard to follow because the lecturer is badly prepared, rambling, or a poor public speaker, and for many other reasons. But the likelihood is that if you are finding it difficult to follow a lecture, it is for some of the other reasons about the nature of the subject given above, rather than just the deficiencies of the lecturer.

Fortunately there are a number of ways in which you can make your task of listening to lectures easier.

Don't expect to learn in your sleep

This may sound obvious, but it is unwise to stay up half the night and then expect to go into a morning philosophy lecture and make sense of everything that is said. Some students assume that if they turn up to the lecture at the right time, listen, and make a few notes on what they hear, that will be enough. But it rarely is. You couldn't learn to play the violin well just by listening to someone playing and talking about the great performers of the past. You need to pick up the instrument and learn how to translate the theory and listening into your own music-making. Learning from lectures should involve learning how to do something as well as learning how other people have performed.

If you heed my advice and make studying philosophy an activity, and don't see yourself as a passive receptacle going into a lecture to be filled up with information, then you will appreciate that engaging actively with what is being said in a lecture requires a certain energy level. It is particularly demanding when you are just finding your bearings. Like most activities, if you practise it and form good habits early on you will make swift progress. It is like learning to drive a car: at first it seems too complicated to be humanly possible, and then a year or two on you will one day find yourself driving well without even thinking about it. If, however, you reinforce bad habits, they can be difficult to break. Ideally you should be in an alert yet relaxed state. Alert enough to think critically about what you are listening to rather than just letting it wash over you; relaxed enough that you can enjoy the experience and not worry too much if you don't understand every word that is uttered.

> The attentive pupil who wishes to be attentive, his eyes riveted on the teacher, his ears open wide, so exhausts himself in playing the attentive role that he ends up by no longer hearing anything.
>
> Jean-Paul Sartre, *Being and Nothingness*

Prepare yourself

For some courses you will have a clearly structured reading requirement, and you should strive to keep abreast of this if you want to follow the lectures. Even if you haven't been given this kind of schedule, it still makes sense to prepare for lectures. One way you can do this is by getting an overview of the topic under discussion. Many lecturers provide study guides to accompany their lectures, and these are very useful sources of such an overview. They usually include suggestions for preliminary reading.

Another painless way to get an overview is to read entries on the topic in two or three dictionaries or encyclopedias of philosophy, such as those recommended at the end of this book. For example, if you are attending your first lecture on scepticism, and don't have any required reading, you might consult the entry under 'scepticism' in a dictionary of philosophy, and then move on to the longer entry in the *Routledge Encyclopedia of Philosophy*, if you have time. You might also consult some general introductory philosophy books. This will give you a good idea about why the topic is an important one, some of the key terms, and perhaps a sense of what is central to a philosophical discussion of the topic. Ten or fifteen minutes of this sort of preparation can save you from perplexity, mind-wandering and boredom in a lecture.

A further way of preparing yourself in a course of lectures is to look back over your notes from the previous lecture in the series. Most professors link their lectures together in a coherent progression. They will usually expect you to remember key points from the previous lecture, and may relate what they are saying to the earlier topic in some detail.

A more thorough preparation for a lecture would involve reading around the subject, if possible being guided by reading lists or study guides provided. Even if you don't understand everything that you read, the lecture may bring it all into focus for you. What you should try to avoid, though, is feeling that because you've read around the subject, you know everything you need to know about it and don't have to listen too closely to the lecture. Most instructors take an angle on the material they ask you to read; if you go in assuming you know precisely what the professor is going to say, then you may miss subtleties of interpretation and criticism.

There may also be seminars in which you can discuss the material covered in the lecture. If you don't have these, then you may find it useful to set up discussion groups with your fellow students. The act of trying to explain an issue or a thinker to someone else can also clarify the issue for you. One of the best ways to understand any subject in depth is to try to teach it to someone else, preferably someone who doesn't know much about the subject in advance, but is prepared to ask difficult questions to get clarification. Many teachers discover how little they really know about some aspect of philosophy when they have to explain it clearly to an intelligent student who has never encountered that idea before. Talking about philosophical ideas, explaining them to your friends, can be a useful part of achieving greater understanding for yourself, as well as making you more aware of the limits of your philosophical understanding, and perhaps even sending you back to your books with a specific question in mind.

Listen for menus

If you attend a meal at a wedding or some other formal occasion, you will probably be given a menu to let you know what you are going to eat and drink. This is useful in a number of ways. It tells you not just what you are about to consume, but also how many courses there will be. The alternative – to have a series of courses served to you without your knowing precisely what you are about to eat, and how many courses there will be – can leave you unsure of whether what you are eating is meant to fill you up or just be an appetiser.

Good teachers will give you the equivalent of a menu at the beginning of their lectures. At some point in the introduction they will let you know what they are going to be talking about and give you some idea of the relative importance of the topics covered. If you want to get the most out of your lectures it is particularly important to pay attention to such menus. Whenever possible jot down some notes to keep the different 'courses' in mind during the lecture. These notes may be useful for revising the topic, but their main function is to help you make sense of what is being said. With such menus professors reveal to you the organising structure of their lectures. Typically they will introduce each section by reminding you where you are on the menu.

Habit 3: Active discussion

Discuss, argue, explore

Discussion is a particularly important component of a philosophical education. It is through discussion that we learn what we know, formulate and explore new ideas, and develop our thinking skills. Until you have had your views challenged and been forced to defend them, you may not have been entirely clear in your mind what you believe and why. Philosophical discussion can also be inspiring and highly enjoyable. Enthusiasm about ideas is contagious.

Traditionally philosophical discussion has taken place face-to-face in informal discussion, in tutorials, in seminars, and in question and answer sessions in lectures. Historically discussion by correspondence has also been important, though present-day philosophers are more likely to use the Internet than rely on the postal service.

There is a great value in discussion in real time, as opposed to the asynchronous discussion that takes place by post or email:* the swiftness of response and intellectual energy of a live discussion can help to focus thought and save wasted effort. If you have an opportunity to discuss philosophy with your teachers or friends, take advantage of it. Although you may feel you understand something well, it is not usually until you have had to state and defend your position against criticism that you realise that your understanding is incomplete. Internet discussions of philosophy have their place too. If they are asynchronous, though, they are more likely to be useful in developing your writing skills than the skills of discussion we have been looking at.

* 'Asynchronous' means not simultaneous. It contrasts with 'live' communication such as face-to-face, or on the telephone.

If you are lucky enough to be taught by a skilled philosopher, there is immense value in witnessing philosophical thought in action. You will see how someone goes about exploring ideas, spotting flaws in others' positions, and defending a case against criticism. There is no more effective way to learn about a particular aspect of philosophy than to have a discussion with someone who understands it thoroughly and sees what is really important. In such a case you will probably want to consolidate what you have learnt by reading further about the topic under discussion. A good philosopher's enthusiasm for the subject can be inspiring and infectious. It may come as a surprise to you, but many philosophers believe that their subject is supremely important. Philosophy really matters, not just as an intellectual game, but in that it focuses on the most profound questions we can ask about our lives and our place in the universe. Philosophers are also renowned for asking the awkward questions that many people would rather not see addressed, questions which can jolt us out of complacency and self-deception. In the two and a half thousand years of its history in the West, philosophy has attracted some of the greatest thinkers who have lived, so it is hardly surprising to find that it has a rich history.

> Most of us live our lives within a very narrow envelope of concerns. We worry about how to pay the mortgage, whether to buy a new car, what to cook for dinner. When we start to think philosophically, we take a step back and look at the wider picture. We start to examine what we have previously taken for granted.
>
> I believe that those who have never taken a step back – who have lived wholly unexamined lives – are not only rather shallow, they're potentially dangerous. One great lesson of the twentieth century is that human beings, no matter how 'civilised', tend to be moral sheep. We are disastrously prone to follow without question the moral lead provided by those around us. From Nazi Germany to Rwanda, you find people blindly going with the flow.
>
> Stephen Law, *The Philosophy Gym*

To an outsider, philosophical discussion can at times seem vicious. No sooner has someone put forward a point, than someone else comes up with a criticism of it. It is as if the contributors to the discussion are intent on undermining each other's positions. And they often are. That is a characteristic feature of a certain kind of philosophical discussion. People put forward ideas and invite criticism of them. Through the criticism, the answering of criticisms, and the rejection of positions which fall prey to serious objections, philosophy progresses. Philosophy thrives on the cut and thrust of this sort of debate, whether it takes place in a seminar room or on the printed or electronic page.

As a participant in this sort of activity, you may at first feel personally attacked. But you shouldn't. Not unless someone is confusing you with your argument. It is a mark of respect for a philosopher as a thinker that other philosophers engage with his or her ideas critically. Once you appreciate that the point of such discussion is to get closer to the truth, to reject ideas which will not stand up to criticism, and replace them with more robust ones, then you should see that a criticism of your argument is not usually meant as a cruel blow to your ego, but as a way of achieving progress in the subject.

> It is the fashion of the present time to disparage negative logic – that which points out weaknesses in theory or errors in practice without establishing positive truths. Such negative criticism would indeed be poor enough as an ultimate result, but as a means to attaining any positive knowledge or conviction worthy the name it cannot be valued too highly.
>
> John Stuart Mill, *On Liberty*

This is not to say that whenever someone raises an objection to what you say, you should simply abandon your beliefs. You should treat objections as stimuli which force you to demonstrate the plausibility of your position, by defending it with examples, reasons and so on.

Studying philosophy is not simply a matter of verbal combat training. It is not a matter of learning to win an argument at all costs. The point of learning the skills of argument, and of engaging with other thinkers' objections is to arrive closer to the truth on any issue, and to make sure that the arguments you are using to defend a position are good arguments. Philosophical argument isn't about persuasion by rhetoric, but a matter of giving good reasons.*

But philosophical discussion need not just be the to and fro of argument and counterargument. Talking about philosophy can involve interpretation, exploration of possibilities, and working together as a group to achieve deeper understanding and insight into the work of a philosopher or a particular topic. Sometimes the point of a discussion is to get someone to see things from a different perspective, to understand why a philosopher is arguing in a particular way, or to appreciate just what it is a philosopher is getting at and why it matters at all. Discussing philosophy need not be negative nit-picking. It can be a creative exchange of ideas, looking for a new way of understanding a topic or applying familiar ways of thinking to new and challenging situations.

Ask questions

Philosophy is sometimes characterised as an activity of asking questions but never arriving at answers. This is in some ways misleading. There is progress in philosophy, not least when we realise that we are asking the wrong questions. But there is also some truth in the idea. Philosophy has its origins in the difficult

---

* Rhetoric is the art of using fine-sounding language rather than argument to persuade.

questions which arise quite naturally out of the human condition: Why are we here? What is reality? How should we live? These are fundamental questions to which there are no easy answers, and probably no complete ones. That doesn't mean that it's a waste of time exploring the questions.

> The value of philosophy is, in fact, to be sought largely in its very uncertainty. The man who has no tincture of philosophy goes through life imprisoned in the prejudices derived from common sense, from the habitual beliefs of his age or nation, and from convictions which have grown up in his mind without the co-operation or consent of his deliberate reason. To such a man the world tends to become definite, finite, obvious; common objects rouse no questions, and unfamiliar possibilities are contemptuously rejected. As soon as we begin to philosophise, on the contrary, we find . . . that even the most everyday things lead to problems to which only very incomplete answers can be given. Philosophy, though unable to tell us with certainty what is the true answer to the doubts which it raises, is able to suggest many possibilities which enlarge our thoughts and free them from the tyranny of custom. Thus, while diminishing our feeling of certainty as to what things are, it greatly increases our knowledge as to what they may be; it removes the somewhat arrogant dogmatism of those who have never travelled into the region of liberating doubt, and it keeps alive our sense of wonder by showing familiar things in an unfamiliar aspect.
>
> Bertrand Russell, *The Problems of Philosophy*

If you aren't prepared to ask difficult and sometimes awkward questions, you are probably studying the wrong subject. In order to get the most out of philosophical discussion you should be prepared to speak up, even at the expense of appearing foolish. Sometimes the simplest questions are the ones which it is most important to ask. There is of course an etiquette of philosophical discussion, and you should be prepared to let others have their say as well as you. But unless you formulate and ask questions yourself it can be difficult to keep philosophy a living subject: you may slip into the kind of passivity that fossilises thought.

> The art of conversation is the art of hearing as well as of being heard.
>
> William Hazlitt, 'On the Conversation of Authors', in *The Plain Speaker*

Whenever you ask a question, listen very carefully to the answer you receive. This may sound like common sense. But it is surprising how often students ask questions, then sit back relieved to have spoken, scarcely hearing the response they get. You should also be prepared to make a response to any answer you get, particularly if something isn't clear. Even if the answer you get reveals to you that you have completely misunderstood what is going on, this can still be useful: without that, you might have persisted in your misunderstanding. And don't be perturbed if you emerge blinking from a seminar or other philosophical discussion feeling that there is nothing you could note down about what was talked about, that no simple important point emerged. Often the process of discussion itself will almost imperceptibly have clarified your ideas about a topic and eliminated possible misunderstandings. At the very least it should have been an opportunity for you to exercise transferable thinking skills and in particular to practise the art of formulating philosophical questions.

Be concise

Nothing stifles philosophical debate so effectively when time is limited as a long-winded question or long-winded answer to a question. It is a mark of clarity of thought that you can express yourself succinctly. Try to keep to the point when you ask a question. This may be difficult at first, when you are grappling with new ideas and new terminology. Sadly some professional philosophers have not yet acquired this skill.

You should also try to keep your responses relatively short. That way there will be time for interaction and further clarification. The point of philosophical discussion is not to trigger a series of mini-lectures, but rather to clarify, criticise and develop arguments, to achieve understanding of a topic, and so on. The great benefit of live discussion is that there is opportunity for feedback, development and interaction of this sort. So be very careful that you do not stifle this.

Habit 4: Active writing

Write

If you are studying for a degree or other qualification in philosophy, you will be assessed primarily on your writing. In your papers and examinations you will be expected to reveal your understanding and insights into philosophical issues and major figures. You will have to argue a case for a conclusion, demonstrating knowledge and understanding of key issues and thinkers. It is through trying to write philosophically that most of us have learnt to be philosophers. Writing, then, serves not just to demonstrate our ability, but also to hone that ability. For many philosophers it is not simply a record of their thoughts, but an activity that is the source of their thoughts. Writing is a kind of thinking. We don't sort out all our ideas and then just transcribe them from our memory. You can write in an unthinking way or you can write in a more active state of mind. Don't think of writing as trotting out what you have learnt. Rather it is part of the activity of thinking about a topic. Often students remark that they haven't understood a topic at all until they began to write about it.

It is possible to study philosophy without ever attempting to write about it, but, like studying philosophy without ever discussing it, this is not to be recommended. It is easy to persuade yourself that you have a clear and thorough understanding of a topic, that your arguments are completely watertight, and so on – until you try to write an essay. Then you realise your limitations. The act of constructing an essay should jolt you into an awareness of the limits of what you know and understand, and of the vulnerability of your position to counterarguments and counter-examples. It is also part of your training in the transferable skills that are at the core of a philosophical education. And, of course, it gives your teacher the opportunity to give you detailed feedback on your progress, reasoning and ideas. Such feedback can give you the sort of insight that will allow you to make significant progress in the subject.

Analyse the question

The questions set for most philosophy papers or examinations fall into three broad categories. These are:

- Invitations to produce a summary followed by a critical discussion
- Comparisons of theories: these often include some assessment of which theory is the most succesful.
- Applications of theories to new situations or cases.

Before beginning to plan your answer, it is a good idea to analyse the question set, making sure you understand what sort of answer your teacher is expecting you to produce.

Summary plus critical discussion questions

Examples

- What is utilitarianism? Does it provide an adequate account of morality?
- What does Rawls mean by 'the original position'? Give a critical analysis of the role it plays in his theory.
- Give a critical account of the main arguments for functionalism in the philosophy of mind.

Summary plus critical discussion questions

- 'The first man who, having enclosed a piece of land, thought of saying "This is mine" and found people simple enough to believe him, was the true founder of civil society.' Jean-Jacques Rousseau. Discuss.
- What is the anthropic principle? Does it provide any insight into the question of God's existence?
- Does the Institutional Theory of art succeed in answering the question 'What is art?'?

Perhaps the commonest question form in philosophy is the summary plus critical discussion question. Here you are invited (either explicitly or implicitly) to lay out an argument or position, and then engage critically with it. Sometimes the two parts of the question are separated and labelled 'a' and 'b'; often they are combined into a single question. Even when the question seems simply to be asking for an interpretation of what a particular philosopher said, this is usually an invitation to engage critically with what the philosopher said, and, perhaps, with what other philosophers have said about that philosopher. Certainly the best answers to this sort of question always do this.

In your answer to this sort of question you should come to a clear conclusion assessing an argument or position summarised. You will be expected to provide a lucid summary of the argument or position, preferably using your own examples to illustrate points. This should be followed by a well-signposted critical discussion of the position. This should not be a polemic, but rather a well-reasoned case for your conclusion, a case which anticipates and meets objections to it. When marking answers to this sort of question, many teachers assign most of the marks for the critical section of the essay.

Comparison questions

Examples

- Does dualism provide a better account of subjective experience than does functionalism?
- Compare and contrast utilitarian and deontological approaches to promise keeping.
- Is the mind a blank slate at birth, or do we have innate knowledge?
- Does virtue theory provide a better account of morality than utilitarianism?
- 'Wrongfully prolonged life can be as tragic an error as wrongfully terminated life.' Joel Feinberg. Discuss.
- Compare and contrast consequentialist and deontological approaches to punishment.

Comparison type questions can be very difficult to answer well, particularly under examination conditions. The difficult decision is whether to compare theories or philosophers point by point, or to opt for summarising one position before beginning the comparison with the other. You need to take a decision on this structural question at the planning stage. If you don't it will be difficult to impose a clear structure on this sort of essay as you write. As with all other varieties of philosophy questions, it is important to come to a conclusion, not just to leave the reader on the fence between positions. This conclusion should be well defended by the reasoning within the essay.

Application questions

Examples

- How would a virtue ethicist go about assessing whether or not an instance of surrogate motherhood was morally acceptable?
- Do Mill's arguments in *On Liberty* help us in assessing whether or not we should censor the Internet?
- Could a murder be a genuine work of art?
- Could a rare plant have rights?

Application questions invite you to show how a particular approach can be applied to a new situation. The process of explaining this allows you to demonstrate your understanding of the theory in question. This sort of question forces you to think through the central aspects of the theory in question. Sometimes examiners introduce deliberately obscure or exotic examples in order to force you to think the issues through for yourself rather than to write up some pre-prepared answer. The idea is that you won't have encountered this particular application before, so you will have to think imaginatively while answering the question. It is important to realise that this is going on with this particular type of question and to avoid instantly rejecting a question because you haven't explicitly covered that application in your study so far.

The division into these three question types is not completely clear cut. Nevertheless the three different types should provide you with a useful way of thinking about the question you are set and how to go about answering it.

Make a plan before you start writing

Most students produce more coherent essays when they begin with a plan, even if that plan gets modified in the process of writing the essay. The plan need only be a broad outline, indicating the main topics of each paragraph. But putting your plan down on paper will probably help you to start writing the essay proper, and save you from writing large sections which end up deleted. For some people the process of writing a plan is also the process of planning the essay itself: it's not as if the plan exists in the mind and then is simply transcribed onto paper. Rather, until the student begins writing a plan, no plan exists.

Start writing sooner rather than later

The process of defending your position in writing is, as we've seen, often a process of thinking things through, not of transcribing thought. Your model should not be that of doing research on a topic and then writing up what you have discovered. The act of writing should stimulate your thought, and perhaps send you back to your books and notes to clarify an issue, or check up on an idea. Some students don't begin to write an essay until very near to its deadline. If you have a tendency to procrastinate about your writing, bear in mind that the process of writing a first draft of an essay is a way of exploring the issues. Don't let your unconscious trick you into thinking you need to do much more research before beginning to write. You will be amazed at how the ideas emerge when you are writing.

> Sit in sun. Sun goes behind cloud. Look at watch. Notice that
> second hand does not always point directly at little marks on dial.
> Sometimes it does, though. Then sometimes it doesn't. Why? Feel
> panic at how quickly life slips by. Get to work.
>
> Nicholson Baker

Leave yourself enough time to rewrite. The process of revision will in most cases greatly improve the end result. If possible, write your draft and set it aside for a few days or more. When you re-read it, it should be more like reading someone else's work than your own, and easier to get a critical distance on it to see where modification is needed.

> Rewriting is part of writing. Few writers are so expert that they can
> produce what they are after on the first try.
>
> William Strunk Jr and E.B. White, *The Elements of Style*

Think about your reader

You should have a clear idea of the sort of person you are writing for. When you are given a philosophy assignment it is not because your instructor wants to learn something that he or she didn't already know about philosophy. Philosophy teachers often do learn from their students, but that isn't their principal aim in setting written work. The assignment is an invitation for you to demonstrate your understanding of the topic, and your ability to construct an argument, synthesising material that you have read or learnt about in lectures and seminars. You should write for an intelligent reader. Don't, however, assume that the reader knows all there is to know about the topic. If you assume the reader's familiarity with everything you have to say, then there is little point in writing the essay at all, and you may be tempted to allude to points rather than make them in a convincing way.

Be precise

Words to take care over

valid/true: In philosophy, the word 'valid' is usually used to describe the structure of an argument. A valid argument is a truth-preserving structure: if you put true premises in then you will get a true conclusion. If one or more of the premises is false, then you may or may not get a true conclusion. Notice that 'true' is used of premises, assertions, facts, statements and so on, but it would be confusing to talk of a 'true' argument. Strictly, 'valid' should not be used for sentences or statements, but only for arguments.

refute/repudiate/deny: if you refute a statement, you demonstrate that it is false. In other words you make an overwhelming case against it. If you repudiate it, you simply deny it.

contradiction/contrary: if one statement contradicts another, both cannot be true, but one must be true. One is the negation of the other. So, for example, 'London is not the capital city of England' contradicts 'London is the capital city of England'. If two statements are contraries, however, though both cannot be true, they both can be false. For example 'cats make the best pets' and 'dogs make the best pets' are contraries: they can't both be true, but they may both be false. Goldfish, for instance, might make the best pets.

disinterested/uninterested: disinterested research is unbiased. 'Uninterested' means not interested, or bored.

imply/infer: premises imply a conclusion. But they don't infer anything. Only people can make inferences. People infer one thing from another.

begs the question/invites the question: someone who begs the question assumes the very point that is at issue. For example, Descartes has been accused of begging the question with his

'Cogito' argument: assuming that all thoughts have thinkers, when in fact that is the very point at issue. There is a colloquial use of 'begs the question' to mean 'invites the question', but this is not how the phrase is used in philosophy.

e.g./i.e.: students frequently confuse these two abbreviations. 'E.g.' always introduces an example: it means 'for example'. 'I.e.' means 'that is'. What follows 'i.e.' should be an explanation of whatever has been described in the first half of the sentence. So, for example (e.g.) I might say that anyone who commits plagiarism, that is (i.e.) cheats by trying to pass someone else's work off as his or her own, is foolish and likely to be caught.

principle/principal: A principle is a guideline or rule. A principal is the head of an American school (hence the mnemonic to avoid confusion: 'Your principal is your pal'). When used as an adjective, 'principal' means main, as in 'the principal objections to Descartes are . . . '. 'Principle' is never an adjective.

Some common spelling mistakes and confusions

- 'arguement' for 'argument'
- 'existance' for 'existence'
- 'their' for 'there' and 'there' for 'their'
- 'its' for 'it's' and 'it's' for 'its': remember that 'its' means 'of it'; 'it's' is short for 'it is'
- 'effect' for 'affect'. The *effect* of something is the result it brings about. *Affect* used as a noun refers to emotion. As a verb, someone can be *affected* by something that happens, or they can also be *affected* in the sense of having very contrived emotional reactions. You can also *effect* a change, i.e. bring about a change.
- 'criterion' is the singular of 'criteria'. Don't write 'a criteria'!
- 'phenomenon' is the singular of 'phenomena'. Don't write 'a phenomena'!

Don't use words too big for the subject. Don't say 'infinitely' when you mean 'very'; otherwise you'll have no word left when you want to talk about something *really* infinite.

C.S. Lewis

Don't just allude to points. Make them!

Example of alluding to a point rather than making it

Essay question: give a critical account of Descartes' argument in his *Meditations*.

1. Descartes' argument in the *Meditations* is vulnerable to the well-known charge of circularity. This charge is fully justified. He can't get round it. A further criticism of Descartes' argument is . . .

Comment: These few sentences allude to a criticism of Descartes' position, but they do not make that criticism clear to the reader. The writer takes it for granted that we all know what he or she is talking about, and doesn't bother to spell it out for us. Nor is there any support for the claim that the charge of circularity 'is fully justified'. This reads like notes for an essay, a compressed version of the real thing. The vital argumentative element where positions are explained and defended or criticised is missing. The mistake may be due to the writer not bothering to explain what he or she knows the reader already knows. But that is to misunderstand completely the genre of the student essay. The whole point of such an essay is to demonstrate your understanding and critical ability, not simply to hint at it.

Example of making a point rather than just alluding to It

2. Descartes' argument in the *Meditations* is vulnerable to the well-known charge of circularity. This is the criticism that the notion of clear and distinct ideas on which so much of his argument rests is dependent on his belief in the existence of a non-deceptive deity. The belief in the non-deceptive deity is based on arguments which themselves rely on the idea that whatever Descartes perceives clearly and distinctly is true. So the structure of the argument that Descartes uses is viciously circular. This is a particularly damaging criticism of Descartes' position, and one that was made in his lifetime. It is like arguing that God must exist because it says that he does in the Bible; and that the Bible must be true because it is the word of God.

Comment: This writer has taken the trouble to spell out what the reader presumably already knew. The point of spelling it out is to demonstrate that the writer understands the topic and can think critically about it. It also gives the writer the opportunity to summarise the position and put the familiar criticism in his or her own words, in this case using an analogy to illustrate the structure of the criticism.

Write clearly

If you can't say it clearly, you don't understand it yourself.

John Searle

One way in which you can demonstrate that you have understood a philosophical idea is to write about it clearly. If your writing is vague and impressionistic, it won't be obvious to your reader that you have a strong grasp of the topic. Don't try to hide behind a smokescreen of long words and high-sounding prose.

Obscurity is the refuge of incompetence.

Robert Heinlein *Stranger in a Strange Land*

Let us, when we sit down to write, take a solemn oath to say exactly what we mean and to say nothing more, to use the simplest words that will serve our purpose, and to use as few of them as we can.

C. E. M. Joad, 'How to Write and How to Write Badly'

It is a safe rule to apply that, when a mathematical or philosophical author writes with a misty profundity, he is talking nonsense.

A. N. Whitehead, *An Introduction to Mathematics*

Some people find writing clearly effortless; others, indeed most of us I suspect, have to work at it. There are some guidelines that might help you achieve a clearer writing style. They aren't firm, unbreakable rules. You may be able to achieve clarity in your writing by other means, but most writers will benefit from reflecting on whether they could express themselves more clearly.

Orwell's six guidelines

The author George Orwell gave some excellent guidelines on clear writing in his essay 'Politics and the English Language' (1946). I recommend that you follow these guidelines when writing philosophy:

- Never use a metaphor, simile or other figure of speech which you are used to seeing in print.
- Never use a long word where a short one will do.
- If it is possible to cut a word out, always cut it out.
- Never use the passive where you can use the active.
- Never use a foreign phrase, a scientific word or a jargon word if you can think of an everyday English equivalent.
- Break any of these rules sooner than say anything outright barbarous.

Avoid convoluted sentence structure

> Have something to say, and say it as clearly as you can. That is the only secret of style.
>
> Matthew Arnold

Philosophy can be difficult enough to read without introducing syntactical difficulties. Some students write in very long and convoluted sentences which add to the difficulty of understanding what they are trying to say. The impression such sentences give is of a rambling unfocused mind. It is true that some great philosophers have chosen to write in this manner. But that isn't what made them great: they are great despite this. When writing within the genre of the student essay, however, it is extremely difficult to demonstrate your understanding of philosophy while writing in this way. Don't expect your assessors to be overwhelmed by your sophistication if you model your sentences on those of Marcel Proust or Hegel.

> A sentence is more likely to be clear if it is a short sentence communicating one thought, or a closely connected range of ideas.
>
> Harold Evans, *Essential English for Journalists, Editors and Writers*

When rewriting your essays, look out for long sentences and ask yourself: Could this be better expressed? Would this sentence be easier to understand if it were divided up? Usually the answer will be: Yes. If you are preparing your paper on a personal computer which has a style and grammar checker, this should alert you when your syntax becomes overcomplex. It should also identify very long sentences; these can be split into shorter ones.

> Clarity, clarity, clarity. When you become hopelessly mired in a sentence, it is best to start fresh; do not try to fight your way through against the terrible odds of syntax. Usually what is wrong

is that the construction has become too involved at some point; the sentence needs to be broken apart and replaced by two or more shorter sentences.

Muddiness is not merely a disturber of prose, it is also a destroyer of life, of hope: death on the highway caused by a badly worded road sign, heartbreak among lovers caused by a misplaced phrase in a well-intentioned letter, anguish of a traveler expecting to be met at a railroad station and not being met because of a slipshod telegram. Think of the tragedies that are rooted in ambiguity, and be clear! When you say something, make sure you have said it. The chances of your having said it are only fair.

William Strunk Jr and E.B. White, *The Elements of Style*

Writing Tip

If you want to write more clearly try reading what you have written out loud before you hand it in. When immersed in writing it is easy to produce convoluted and unreadable sentences. It is quite simple to spot the sentences which need to be cut or reworded when you hear them read out loud.

Make a case

The most important advice about essay writing is this: make a case. In philosophy, as in most subjects, the point of writing is to make a case for a conclusion.

If the question you were asked was a direct question, such as 'Does Descartes succeed in bringing all his former beliefs into doubt?', then your conclusion should contain a direct answer, preferably using the key words from the question. So in this example, I would expect the conclusion of a good essay to include a sentence beginning either 'Despite his expressed intentions, Descartes does not succeed in bringing all his former beliefs into doubt . . .' or, perhaps, 'Descartes does succeed in bringing all his former beliefs into doubt'. The rest of the essay should contain arguments and illustrations which support this conclusion, and rule out alternative interpretations. The arguments and illustrations should build up to the conclusion.

With more open-ended styles of question, such as 'Discuss critically Descartes' pre-emptive scepticism', your whole answer should still support whatever conclusion you arrive at. Again you should pick up on key words in the question in your conclusion to make it absolutely clear to the reader that you have answered the question you were set, and not simply provided a vague discussion of a related topic.

Making a case usually requires a certain amount of summary. You cannot begin to answer a question about the success or failure of Descartes' pre-emptive scepticism without spelling out what this scepticism involves. In this case you would need to explain what is meant by 'pre-emptive' in this context; this would include explaining that Descartes was not himself a sceptic, but rather used sceptical arguments to demonstrate that some of his beliefs were immune to the strongest forms of scepticism. Yet most philosophy essays demand far more of the writer than just clear exposition of other people's ideas. Most philosophy essays require you to write critically about the ideas you set out. What this means in practice is that you need to present arguments for and against a position. This is not a neutral process of laying out all the available positions before your reader and letting him or her choose between them. Rather you should be building up to your main conclusion through your critical engagement with the various arguments. So, for example, in answering the question 'Does Descartes succeed in bringing all his former beliefs into doubt in his first *Meditation*?' you would first lay out clearly the process by which Descartes calls his former beliefs into question, making sure that you restrict yourself to the arguments of the first *Meditation*, which is the question's focus. Assuming that you wanted to conclude that he does not bring *all* his former beliefs into doubt, you should pinpoint which of his former beliefs are not challenged by his method. This would involve references back to the text, use of your own examples, and argument. On the basis of your discussion of these beliefs, you should then draw your overall conclusion, picking up on the words used in the question.

Make a point, back it up, show its relevance

One useful way of building the paragraphs of an essay is to make sure that each one contains these three ingredients:

- A point clearly made
- Some sort of evidence or argument to back it up
- An indication of how your point is relevant to the question asked. This should clinch the point you have made. It is in a sense the punchline of each paragraph, the answer to the question 'So what?'

Writing tip

At the end of each paragraph you write, ask yourself the question 'So what?' Your answer to this question should relate what you have just written back to the question. You should not stray from the question asked. This is particularly important when writing examination essays. Philosophical writing requires discipline: keep everything relevant. Don't be sidetracked. No red herrings.

This is not the only way to construct a paragraph, but it is one that works well for philosophy essays:

An example of a three-part paragraph

If you were asked to give a critical account of utilitarianism you might, once you had explained what utilitarianism is, construct a paragraph using the three-part structure just outlined. You could begin:

> One major criticism of utilitarianism is that it appears to justify some actions which are intuitively immoral.

Comment: This is your point clearly made. The first few words also indicate to your reader that you are moving on from exposition to critical engagement with utilitarianism, and that this paragraph is going to deal with one criticism of the theory.

You might then back this up with an example to illustrate your point:

> For instance, imagine a healthy but depressed person walking into a hospital ward. In this ward one patient needs a kidney transplant, another a heart transplant, another a bone marrow transplant, another a lung transplant, two more corneal transplants, another blood transfusion, and so on. All the patients would be delighted to be given their transplants, no matter how the organs were acquired. Their happiness would far outweigh any happiness of which the healthy person is capable. It seems that a utilitarian would have to say that it would be right to remove the healthy but depressed individual's organs by force because this act would result in greater overall happiness than any other available course of action. Yet this action would be morally repugnant to most of us.

Comment: This development of the paragraph backs up the point made in the opening sentence. It provides an example of the type of morally repugnant action that utilitarianism seems to justify.

Your reader should never be left asking 'So what?' To clinch the point just made, you might add:

> This shows that utilitarianism justifies actions which go strongly against most people's moral intuitions.

Comment: This sentence indicates that you are answering the question set, not least because you pick up on the word 'utilitarianism'.

You might then want to trail your next paragraph, in which you will be going on to present a utilitarian response to this sort of criticism:

> A utilitarian, however, might well respond that this sort of case is so far-fetched that it is unlikely to be met with in real life.

Comment: This final sentence of your paragraph leads into the next paragraph in which you might go on to spell out a utilitarian response to the criticism you have just made, back it up with argument, and then make clear that the paragraph is relevant to the question set. You might want to use this sentence as the first of the subsequent paragraph rather than the last one as here.

Keep it relevant

Every sentence that you write in a philosophy essay should be relevant to the question asked. If you find a passage that is tangential, cut it. You dilute your essay by including any irrelevant material no matter how accurate, well expressed, or insightful it is. For example, it can be very tempting to begin an essay on

Hume's theory of causation with the line 'David Hume was born in Scotland in 1711', but unless you want to make a particular point about his theory of causation being linked to his Scottishness or the date of his birth, this is irrelevant to your answer. If you find that you have written an introductory paragraph which consists mainly of irrelevant biographical information, cross it out. It is surprising how often student essays come into focus only in the second paragraph.

Many books and encyclopedia articles on particular philosophers begin with some sort of biographical summary. It can be tempting to mirror these in your own assignment writing. In most cases, though, you will be writing an answer to a specific question, not being asked to provide a summary of someone's life and works. You will only dilute your answer by including irrelevant facts. You may also disguise the structure of your essay. You will not get any credit for irrelevant facts, no matter how interesting they are. Nor should unnecessary words have any place in your writing.

> Vigorous writing is concise. A sentence should contain no unnecessary words, a paragraph no unnecessary sentences, for the same reason that a drawing should have no unnecessary lines and a machine no unnecessary parts. This requires not that the writer make all sentences short, or avoid all detail and treat subjects only in outline, but that every word tell.
>
> William Strunk Jr and E.B. White, *The Elements of Style*

Resist the temptation to begin an essay with a dictionary definition of a key term. Essays which open with sentences such as 'The Oxford English Dictionary defines "scepticism" as . . .' rarely get good marks. Ordinary dictionaries very rarely have anything important or interesting to contribute to the definition of philosophical terms. More often, the philosophical use of a term differs sufficiently from normal use of it for any dictionary definition to be seriously misleading and somewhat off the point. It is a common, yet rather lazy-minded approach to begin every essay with a dictionary definition. It is far better to turn to one or more philosophical dictionaries for definitions of philosophical terms.

A phrase you can do without

> The phrase 'the fact that' can often be replaced with 'since' or 'though' or a more succinct phrase: e.g. 'the fact that Locke believed a child's mind to be a blank slate coloured all his thought' is better expressed as 'Locke's belief that a child's mind was a blank slate coloured all his thought'.

Use paragraphs as units of thought not length

One of the easiest ways to make the structure of your writing clear is to use paragraphs effectively. The reader of your essay will be glad of help in understanding what you are trying to say. There is no ideal length in terms of words or sentences of a paragraph. The right length of each paragraph is determined by its content. If you are using paragraphs wisely, they should reveal when you have moved on to a new idea. Try to keep one main idea per paragraph. Avoid a series of one-sentence paragraphs as this clearly indicates that you are not exploring any issue in sufficient depth.

Include signposts

I have already mentioned the value of signposts when you are reading philosophy. It is a good idea when rewriting an essay to look at the first sentence of each of your paragraphs and to consider whether or not it indicates the main point expressed in that paragraph. Sentences which begin with phrases such as the following are extremely useful to the reader: 'A second serious criticism of X is . . .', 'A possible counterexample to the argument just set out is . . .' etc.

If you follow this advice, it should be possible to discern the structure of your essay simply by looking at the first sentence of each paragraph.

Study tip

If you want to check that you are using signpost sentences effectively, try copying out the first sentence of each paragraph of an essay you have already written and then see whether or not the argument structure of your essay is communicated through good use of signposts. If it isn't, you could try rewriting each first sentence.

Use quotations sparingly

Generally in philosophy you should not quote long passages from the work of other philosophers or their critics unless you are going to give a detailed analysis of those passages. Some students produce collages of quotations that fail to demonstrate their own under-standing of the topic under discussion. A good paraphrase is often much more effective in making a point than a direct quotation. When you do quote a passage, make sure you acknowledge the source clearly – otherwise you may get accused of plagiarism (see p. 71). Quote when the philosopher's language is distinctive in a way that would not be captured by a paraphrase. For instance, if you were explaining Thomas Hobbes' beliefs about life in the state of nature, then it would be appropriate to quote his famous lines about the life of man under those conditions being 'solitary, poor, nasty, brutish and short'. But unless you were going to analyse the passage sentence by sentence, it would not usually be appropriate to quote the whole passage from his *Leviathan* in which these lines occur. Similarly, you might want to quote John Locke's contention that the mind of a child at birth is a blank slate, or as he puts it a 'tabula rasa' on which various ideas become written. In both cases, quoting demonstrates your familiarity with the text. Anyone can quote large chunks of a philosophical text; it takes skill to select short appropriate quotations that demonstrate both your knowledge of the text and your understanding of it. Don't copy my use of quotations in this book: remember I'm not writing a philosophy essay here.

Consider counterarguments

I have stressed that you should make a case for a conclusion in your philosophical writing. This does not mean, however, that your case should be one-sided. Whenever you defend a position, anticipate possible objections to it and pre-empt them. Give the strongest arguments against your position and demonstrate why they don't work. Show that you have appreciated the other side of the argument, but that objections, counterarguments and counter-examples can all be met and dealt with by your approach. If you consider only the arguments in favour of your conclusion, you give yourself too easy a ride: the reader of the essay (who is likely to be an *active* reader) will no doubt think up the arguments on the other side and will have no evidence that you are able to answer them. Your aim is not to produce an impassioned and opinionated polemic, but rather a reasoned and well-argued piece of writing, one that weighs arguments on either side of an issue and comes to a clear conclusion on the matter addressed by the question.

Don't plagiarise

plagiarise: to steal from (the writings or ideas of another).
Chambers Dictionary, 1998

You should avoid plagiarism. If you deliberately pass off someone else's work as your own then you are engaging in a deception that is fairly obviously immoral. But even if you accidentally give the impression that you are passing off someone else's work as your own, you are still likely to be classed as a plagiarist. Most academic institutions punish plagiarists very severely.

There are at least two possible justifications for this treatment. First, those assessing you may feel it dangerous to give anyone the benefit of the doubt in such circumstances: others may commit plagiarism deliberately and then get off lightly by professing that it was accidental plagiarism.

A second justification, more interesting philosophically, is to point out that as a student you take on certain role responsibilities. Just as medical doctors and school teachers take on responsibilities associated with their professions, so students, when they begin to submit work for assessment, are bound by an implicit contract. One of their resulting responsibilities is not just to avoid deliberate plagiarism, but also to avoid the kind of laziness or sloppiness about note-taking from books that can result in accidentally giving the impression that you are attempting to pass off someone else's work as your own.

Online plagiarism

A relatively recent phenomenon is online plagiarism. Some students have discovered that there are websites which specialise in providing pre-written essays on philosophical topics. Although, presumably for legal reasons, creators of such sites claim that their websites are only intended to help students focus their own work, this is not how they are being used. Even if you are tempted to use such sites in a legitimate way, as sources of ideas rather than chunks of prose to cut and paste into your own essay, you should be extremely careful to avoid the charge of plagiarism. It is always safer to include references to the sources of your ideas. Be warned that many of those marking essays use quite sophisticated software to identify copied and uncredited material. And you can never be certain that none of your fellow students has used the same source as you.

More importantly, doing philosophy is very different from cutting and pasting together an essay. If you are concerned only about the mark you get for an assignment, no matter how you achieve it, then you have completely missed the point of studying philosophy.

Plagiarism, paraphrase and exposition: five examples

1 If the sceptic is right, then each of us is in an important way detached from the world around us. You know nothing about the world out there. You have no reason at all to believe that you inhabit a world of trees, houses, cats, dogs, mountains and cars. And you have no reason at all to think that you are surrounded by other people. For all you know, your entire world – including all the people in it – is merely virtual.

Comment: This is a direct yet unacknowledged quotation from

p. 53 of Stephen Law's excellent introduction to philosophy, *The Philosophy Files* (London: Orion, 2000). The only difference between what is written above and what is in the book is that I have removed two comments which are in parentheses in the original. If I had written this as a paragraph in a philosophy essay without quotation marks or acknowledgement of its source , it would be a clear case of plagiarism. It would still be counted as plagiarism even if I had simply forgotten to put in the quotation marks, though I might not be so culpable, it is unlikely that anyone marking this would give me the benefit of the doubt.

> **2** Imagine for the sake of argument that the sceptic is right. In that case each of us is in an important way detached from the external world. We know nothing of the world out there. We have no reason at all to believe that there are trees, houses, cats, mountains etc. For all you know, your whole world, including everyone in it, is a virtual one.

Comment: Again this is plagiarism, though not in such a blatant form as in the first passage. Although I have paraphrased the original, the syntax, examples and sentence structure are so similar to the original that the derivation is still obvious. Furthermore, there is no acknowledgement whatsoever of the original source. The only plausible justification for such paraphrase would be to avoid the charge that it is simply an unacknowledged quotation – there is no philosophical justification for simply rewriting a passage in slightly different words.

> **3** Stephen Law says that if the sceptic is right, 'then each of us is in an important way detached from the world around us.' Then we have no reason to believe that we inhabit a world of 'trees, houses, cats, dogs, mountains and cars'. And we have no reason to believe in the existence of other people. For all you know 'your entire world – including all the people in it' is merely virtual.

Comment: This time, although the source of the quotation is acknowledged, this passage is simply a collage of quotations – some marked by quotation marks, others not. Although this might escape the charge of plagiarism, it is still a very weak way of summarising a passage and demonstrates no understanding of the passage summarised. The main ideas are simply parroted. Most philosophy essays will involve a certain amount of summary and exposition of others' ideas. The art of summary, however, is not an art of cut and paste. It involves explanation and, preferably, the use of some fresh examples rather than the reuse of just those in the original text.

> 4 In *The Philosophy Files*, Stephen Law summarises the sceptical position: 'each of us is in an important way detached from the world around us. You know nothing about the world out there' (p. 53). Most importantly, he emphasises that a sceptic has no reason for believing in the existence of other people. Our experiences, which seem to be of other people, may be misleading. We may in fact be looking at holograms, or else be plugged into a virtual reality machine which creates the illusion of our seeing, hearing, touching, feeling and smelling other people.

Comment: This passage both summarises and explains the ideas in Law's paragraph. It also acknowledges the source of the quotation, and puts the idea that we may be plugged into a virtual reality machine in his or her own words. This is not a case of plagiarism, but of the sort of exposition that would be appropriate in a philosophy essay.

> 5 Most of us, most of the time are convinced that the world we perceive with our senses exists and is more or less as it appears to us. Sceptics challenge our complacency about this. They argue that we have no more reason to believe that such things as walls, tables, chairs, feet and goldfish actually exist than that they don't. All these things may be imaginary. Furthermore, other people may

not exist. Sceptics entertain that what we take to be experience may be created by someone manipulating us: we may simply be plugged into a highly sophisticated virtual reality machine, even if we don't realise this is the case. The key point is that for the sceptic there is no more reason to believe that things are as they seem than that they aren't.

Comment: This passage addresses the same ideas as the quotation from Stephen Law, but it does so in a way that makes clear that I have understood the ideas being expressed and have made them my own to such a degree that there is probably no need to indicate in the main text that they were inspired by the passage in Law's book (though it would be appropriate in such circumstances to include a reference to Law's book in the bibliography). If in doubt, though, it is always safer to include mention of the original source, and you are unlikely ever to be penalised for this.[*]

Avoid autobiography

A common mistake when writing philosophy papers is to include autobiographical confessions. These usually begin with phrases like 'My personal opinion is' or 'I have always felt that'. These kinds of personal revelations are seldom if ever relevant to making a case. Typically they are subjective assertions which are not backed

[*] For this reason I should mention that the idea for laying out examples of plagiarism in this way came from a handout written in 1989 by Richard Dennis of the University College London Geography department, though I have used my own examples and have included more explanation of them than he does.

up or argued for in any way. They are also redundant. If you are sincere, the whole of your essay will express your own position on the topic under discussion: the conclusion you arrive at will be one you endorse. You don't need to conclude an essay 'I believe that Descartes does indeed call all his former beliefs into doubt'; the words 'I believe that' are redundant and should be struck out. The conclusion is *your* conclusion. If you preface your conclusion with words such as 'In my opinion' or 'It is my firm belief that' you undermine any argument that you have used to make your case and imply that your conclusion is simply a profession of belief rather than the product of a reasoned analysis of the issue.

Phrases to avoid when writing philosophy

'In my opinion . . .'

'I believe that . . .'

'Personally, . . .'

'I have always felt that . . .'

'It seems to me that . . .'

'My personal opinion, for what it's worth, is . . .'

'I feel strongly that . . .'

'In my humble opinion . . .'

'On a personal note . . .'

'From my point of view . . .'

Be original

Many students beginning philosophy find it hard to see how they can produce anything original. It's not that they want to pass off someone else's work as their own. But they can't understand how in the first few years of studying the subject they could possibly hope to say something that isn't obviously derivative.

> When you steal from one author, it's plagiarism; if you steal from
> many, it's research.
>
> Wilson Mizner

It is important to realise that you are not being asked to philosophise at the level of Wittgenstein or Quine. You don't have to
come up with startlingly new theories when writing philosophy
essays. Your originality can be in the way you set out familiar
arguments. It can also lie in the way you combine a variety of
arguments from different sources (always, of course, acknowledging
those sources). The main aim is to show that you have understood
the material you are studying and are thinking critically about it,
not simply parroting it. A parrot doesn't understand the words it
parrots. You need to find a way of showing that you are not in the
same position. Here are some strategies for being original when
studying philosophy.

Think up your own examples

One of the easiest ways to demonstrate that you are thinking for
yourself is to use your own examples. If you were writing an essay
about Descartes' *Meditations*, you might think up further examples
to illustrate the points Descartes makes. When explaining why he
did not want to trust his senses absolutely, he uses the example of
a stick in water looking bent when it is straight. Perhaps you could
come up with several other misleading sensory experiences to
make the point more emphatically, and to demonstrate that you are
thinking about the issue. You might mention the fact that the moon
looks bigger when it is low on the horizon, even though it remains
the same size, or the fact that cold objects can feel as if they are
wet. As well as demonstrating your understanding of the point in

question, using your own examples is a way of being more creative in your philosophical writing. Your readers will appreciate imaginative and appropriate examples in place of the clichéd examples they have seen many times before.

Include a bibliography

Unless explicitly advised not to, you should include a bibliography of works consulted in writing your essay. The usual convention is to indicate book titles by underlining or italicising. Article and chapter titles are given within inverted commas. Website addresses are usually given within these brackets: < >. Include the date you accessed the website as there is no guarantee that the content online will remain the same indefinitely.

There are several acceptable conventions about giving references, and you should take advice from your teacher. In the absence of such advice, the forms given below are acceptable.

Books

Warburton, N. (2004) *Philosophy: The Basics*, 4th edn, London: Routledge.

Articles

Warburton, N. (1998) 'Freedom to Box', *Journal of Medical Ethics*, 24(1): 56–60.

Webpages

<http://www.open.ac.uk/Arts/philos/warburton.htm>

The point of including such a bibliography is to acknowledge your sources, and so avoid charges of plagiarism. It will also be useful if you refer back to the essay at a later date, by which time you may have forgotten which books you used in writing it.

Use the Internet, but use it wisely

If you use the Internet to research your philosophy paper, you should always provide details of the sites used in your bibliography to avoid the charge of plagiarism. You should also remember that while most books which make it onto the shelves of a university library are above a certain threshold of academic respectability, the Internet gives you access to many thousands of poorly researched and idiosyncratic sites as well as many thousands of useful ones. Just because a site's author purports to be giving you a clear analysis of what Descartes really meant, it doesn't follow that the interpretation is tied in any way to the text of Descartes' work. The author may have the sketchiest of understandings of Descartes' philosophy and may end up seriously misleading you, perhaps even deliberately.

You can minimise the dangers of wasting your time with such sites by paying particular attention to the sources you use on the Internet. If you find one reputable site, it may well have links to others which have been vetted by the author of that site. Some universities provide lists of reputable sites that they recommend to their students on particular topics. These content-sorted gateways are the best route to suitable research materials on the Web. For some further suggestions about where you can find interesting and accurate philosophical information on the Internet, see the section at the end of this book.

Preparing for examinations in philosophy

Revision

Active revision is the key to performing well in examinations. Good preparation is the foundation of good performance. It is easy to while away many an hour grazing over revision notes and nodding off over set texts. But this is unlikely to be the most effective use of your time. You need to prepare for the activity you will be judged on. What is that activity? In most cases you will be expected to write three or more essays in three hours or less. The marks you get will not be directly proportional to the number of hours you put into revision. There is nothing mysterious about what you need to do in order to get good grades in philosophy. The best marks go to clear, well-argued essays that are focused on the particular question set and which make a good case for the conclusion arrived at and include some degree of originality.

Almost everything already mentioned about writing good essays generally applies, with the exception of giving references and bibliographies – you are not usually expected to provide full bibliographical information under examination conditions.

Think of revision as not simply looking back over what you have done, but rather as preparation for what you will have to do. This sounds obvious, but once you begin taking the easy route of just glancing over what you noted down about your course, you can easily be seduced into believing that that is all the preparation relevant to the examination.

Write practice essays

The painful truth is that the best way to prepare to write under examination conditions is to practise writing timed essays. If you were preparing for a marathon, you wouldn't be surprised to learn that the best training you could do was to run long distances. That's not the only training you should do, but unless your training includes some long runs, you are unlikely to make the distance. But because writing timed essays is a lot more gruelling than skimming over old notes, most students shy away from the obvious truth that writing essays against the clock is what you need to practise. Set aside an hour, take a question from a past examination paper, and try to write a legible, coherent, well-argued essay in response. Even if the result is a mess, it is far better to get this bad essay out of the way than risk producing it in the actual examination. What you will very quickly discover is that it is very difficult to plan and write a complex philosophy essay under these conditions. So keep it simple and focused.

There is no room whatsoever for digression. Exposition of ideas takes time. Thinking up relevant illustrative examples takes time. Addressing arguments and counterarguments takes time. With all this going on, if you have to write by hand, you will probably be struggling to keep your handwriting legible. Yet if it is not easy to read, the marker may not recognise how well argued your work really is. If you do have to write by hand in the examination and you usually use a word processor to write, then you may have to work on the physical preparation of writing legibly at speed as well as sorting out the intellectual side.

Write practice outlines

If you really can't bring yourself to write practice essays, then writing practice outline answers to specific questions is another good way of engaging actively with what you know. It forces you to structure your ideas as potential examination answers, and can be a very effective way of discovering gaps in your understanding of material. When you write practice outlines, make sure that you really are answering the question set, and not just summarising your thoughts on a topic. Within the outline your angle on the question and the conclusion you are arguing towards, should be obvious.

Write examination questions

Put yourself in the position of the person writing the examination paper. For any topic there are relatively few questions that can be asked. Try writing examination-style questions yourself, using past examination papers as a guide. You can use the questions you concoct for writing practice essays and practice outlines. Even if you don't get round to doing this, the activity forces you to come at the topic with a critical eye and, again, is part of active preparation. Whether writing practice essays, outlines or questions, whenever you reveal a gap in your understanding, you will be able to go back to your notes and reference books with a specific question that needs answering, and some motivation to answer it.

Be prepared to think

It is particularly important with philosophy that you go in to the examination expecting to have to think. Don't expect to regurgitate what you have learnt undigested. You will have to draw together relevant elements of what you have learnt to make a coherent case for a conclusion that answers the question set. If you begin the examination with your head stuffed with memorised quotations and preconceptions about what you are going to be asked, then you may fail to answer the actual questions in front of you and end up answering the questions you would have liked to have appeared. You have to be prepared to think things through in the actual examination room. Often the examiners will have deliberately thought up questions that they know you won't have anticipated simply to force you to think about and apply your ideas rather than to repeat your revision. If you have the appropriate frame of mind, such questions shouldn't disconcert you: they should challenge you to organise what you know in a new way. If you are well prepared, answering such questions even under examination conditions, can be stimulating. You will find that as you write you are thinking about the material in new ways. Some students of philosophy have even said that the subject didn't really crystallise for them until they found themselves thinking things through as they wrote examination essays. If you prepare well, this process of thinking clearly about a topic under time pressure can even be exhilarating. Remember, an education in philosophy should be an education in thinking for yourself. Ultimately, what you take away from your academic studies shouldn't be just a grade and a few fading notes. If you put the principles in this book into practice you should be a better thinker and a better writer than when you began studying the subject.

Conclusion

This book is deliberately short because the best way to develop your philosophy skills is to practise them rather than to read about practising them. Philosophy can be a challenging subject, but it can also be intensely enjoyable to study when approached as an activity. The transferable skills of clarity of thought and writing are some of the most valuable ones education can impart.

If you have found this book useful or have ideas about how I could improve it in subsequent editions, please email me at n.warburton@open.ac.uk

Further reading

Writing clearly

William Strunk Jr and E.B. White (2000) *The Elements of Style*, 4th edn, Boston, MA: Allyn and Bacon.

Study skills

Ellie Chambers and Andrew Northedge (1997) *The Arts Good Study Guide*, Milton Keynes: The Open University.

Writing philosophy essays

Anne Michaels Edwards (2000) *Writing to Learn: An Introduction to Writing Philosophical Essays*, New York: McGraw-Hill.

Joel Feinberg (2002) *Doing Philosophy: A Guide to the Writing of Philosophy Papers*, 2nd edn, New York: Wadsworth.

A.P. Martinich (1996) *Philosophical Writing*, 2nd edn, Oxford: Blackwell.

Zachary Seech (2000) *Writing Philosophy Papers*, 3rd edn, New York: Wadsworth.

Critical thinking

Anne Thomson (2002) *Critical Reasoning: A Practical Introduction*, 2nd edn, London: Routledge.

Nigel Warburton (2000) *Thinking from A to Z*, 2nd edn, London: Routledge.

Anthony Weston (2000) *A Rulebook for Arguments*, Indianapolis, IN: Hackett.

General introductions to philosophy

Simon Blackburn (1999) *Think: A Compelling Introduction to Philosophy*, Oxford: Oxford University Press.

Edward Craig (2002) *Philosophy: A Very Short Introduction*, Oxford: Oxford University Press.

Stephen Law (2003) *The Philosophy Gym: 25 Short Adventures in Thinking*, London: Review.

Nigel Warburton (2001) *Philosophy: The Classics*, 2nd edn, London: Routledge.

Nigel Warburton (2004) *Philosophy: The Basics*, 4th edn, London: Routledge.

Nigel Warburton (ed.) (2004) *Philosophy: Basic Readings*, 2nd edn, London: Routledge.

Dictionaries and encyclopedias of philosophy

There are many dictionaries of philosophy available. I have listed the ones I find most useful here:

Robert Audi (ed.) (1999)*The Cambridge Dictionary of Philosophy*, 2nd edn, Cambridge: Cambridge University Press.

Simon Blackburn (1994) *The Oxford Dictionary of Philosophy*, Oxford: Oxford University Press.

Anthony Flew and Stephen Priest (eds) (2002) *A Dictionary of Philosophy*, London: Pan.

Ted Honderich (ed.) (1995) *The Oxford Companion to Philosophy*, Oxford: Oxford University Press.

The best long encyclopedia currently available is the *Routledge Encyclopedia of Philosophy* edited by Edward Craig. This contains substantial articles on all the important topics in philosophy. Most good libraries will have this in their reference section, or have an online subscription at <www.rep.routledge.co.uk>. The *Stanford Encyclopedia of Philosophy* is also worth consulting: it is available free online (see next section).

Internet resources

There are numerous philosophy resources available on the Internet. You should, however, use them with caution. They are not all reliable. Many personal sites are factually and philosophically misleading. One very useful and reliable resource is the *Stanford Encyclopedia of Philosophy* available free online at <www.plato. stanford.edu>. One of the most useful websites for philosophers is at <www.epistemelinks.com>. This consists of a wide range of philosophy sites sorted by category. The sites for *The Philosophers' Magazine* and *Philosophy Now*, details of which are given below, also include useful links to other philosophy sites. My own website is at <http://www.open.ac.uk/Arts/philos/warburton.htm>. I also share a website with the philosopher Stephen Law at <http://www. thinking-big.co.uk>.

Philosophy magazines

Think, edited by Stephen Law, published three times a year, is the Royal Institute of Philosophy's journal. It is written for a general readership. Further details are available from www. royalinstitutephilosophy.org/think. *The Philosophers' Magazine* and *Philosophy Now* are both accessible and interesting. Further information about these two magazines, together with links to other sites can be found at <www.philosophers.co.uk> and <www. philosophynow.org>.

4th Edition
Philosophy: The Basics

Nigel Warburton,
The Open University

Now in its fourth edition, Nigel
Warburton's best-selling book gently
eases the reader into the world of
philosophy. Each chapter considers a
key area of philosophy, explaining and
exploring the basic ideas and themes.

• What is philosophy?

• Can you prove God exists?

• Is there an afterlife?

• How do we know right from wrong?

• Should you ever break the law?

• Is the world really the way you think it is?

• How should we define Freedom of Speech?

• Do you know how science works?

• Is your mind different from your body?

• Can you define art?

For the fourth edition, Warburton has added new sections to several
chapters, revised others and brought the further reading sections up
to date. If you've ever asked what is philosophy, or whether the
world is really the way you think it is, then this is the book for you.

Hb: 0-415-32772-5
Pb: 0-415-32773-3

For all your A Level
Philosophy study needs…

Philosophy
for AS and A2

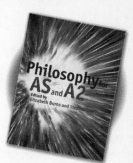

Edited by **Elizabeth Burns**
and **Stephen Law**,
Heythrop College, London

**'Philosophy is becoming ever more
popular as both an AS and A2 level
subject. This comprehensive survey of
major philosophical themes in the
syllabus fulfils a real need, and will be an invaluable tool for study.'**
– *Professor Roger Trigg, Founding Chair of the British Philosophical
Association*

Philosophy for AS and A2 is the definitive textbook for students of Advanced
Subsidiary or Advanced Level courses, structured directly around the
specification of the AQA - the only exam board to offer these courses. A
team of experienced teachers devote a chapter each to the six themes
covered by the syllabus:

AS	A2
• Theory of Knowledge	• Philosophy of Mind
• Moral Philosophy	• Political Philosophy
• Philosophy of Religion	• Philosophy of Science

Each of the six themed chapters includes:

• A list of key concepts, to introduce students to the topic
• Bite-size sections corresponding to the syllabus topics
• Actual exam questions from previous years
• Suggested discussion questions to promote debate
• Text-boxes with helpful summaries, case-studies and examples
• An annotated further-reading list directing students towards the best
  articles, books and websites
• A comprehensive glossary, providing a handy reference point

There is a final chapter on essay writing and exam preparation, designed to
help students get to grips with the examination board requirements.

Hb: 0-415-33562-0
Pb: 0-415-33563-9